Poptropica® English

STUDENT BOOK 2

Tropical Island

CB080293

Linnette Ansel Erocak • Laura Miller
Series advisor: David Nunan

Pearson Education Limited
Edinburgh Gate
Harlow
Essex CM20 2JE
England
and Associated Companies throughout the world.

Poptropica English

Based on the work of Linnette Ansel Erocak

The rights of Laura Miller, and Linnette Erocak to be identified as authors of this work have been asserted by them in accordance with the Copyright, Designs and Patents Act 1988.

Stories on pages 16, 26, 38, 48, 60, 70, 82, and 92 by Catherine Prentice. The rights of Catherine Prentice to be identified as authors of this work have been asserted by them in accordance with the Copyright, Designs and Patents Act 1988.

Phonics syllabus and activities by Rachel Wilson

Editorial and project management by hyphen

First published 2015
Second impression 2023
ISBN: 978-1-292-39250-9

Set in Fiendstar 17/21pt

Printed in Slovakia by Neografia

Illustrators: Humberto Blanco (Sylvie Poggio Artists Agency), Anja Boretzki (Good Illustration), Scott Burroughs (Deborah Wolfe Ltd), Eva Byrne (The Bright Agency), Adam Clay, Lee Cosgrove, Leo Cultura, Joelle Dreidemy (The Bright Agency), Tom Heard (The Bright Agency), Marek Jagucki, Sue King (Plum Pudding Illustration) Daniel Limon (Beehive Illustration), Stephanine Lau, Yam Wai Lun, Katie McDee, Bill McGuire (Shannon Associates), Baz Rowell (Beehive Illustration), Mark Ruffle, Jackie Stafford, Olimpia Wong and Teddy Wong

Picture Credits: The Publishers would like to thank the following for their kind permission to reproduce their photographs: (Key: b-bottom; c-center, l-left; r-right; t-top)
123RF.com: 36/2, akulamatiau 41/1 (left), Jacek Chabraszewski 33 (girl), 40 (e), goodluz 28 (e), Sergey Kolesnikov 111/1, Dmytrii Minishev 93br, stockyimages 40 (h), Waroot Tangtumsatid 84/3, Gary Tognoni 110 (a); Alamy Images: DP RM 61/4, Jose Gi 111/3, Keith Morris 30tr, Photo Japan 111/2, Olga Volodina 30tc; Comstock Images: 94/4; Fotolia.com: babimu 93tc, Bernad 40 (i), brites_99 41/3 (left), Buriy 68/2, Jacek Chabraszewski 41/4 (right), Yanik Chauvin 62/5, Gennaro Coretti 36/5, Chepko Danil 94/3, Dar1930 93tl, demidoff 80/2, Mehmet Dilsiz 86/2, Joerg Dirmeitis 36/4, Daria Filiminova 28 (baby), fotofac 76l, Fotolyse 50bc, Gelpi 72/1, giideon 94/5, Scott Griessel 86/1, Mat Hayward 36/8, highwaystarz 107b, imagedb.com 41/4 (left), imagesetc 50bl, 71/1, indigolotos 80/10, iofoto 25r, Eric Isselée 58/2, katrinaelena 28 (a), lculig 80/6, Liaurinko 80/7, Pavel Losevsky 40 (c), mayakova 30b, Monkey Business 107t, monticellllo 68/7, 71/2, Natika 61/3, 68/5, 74/3, 74/4, Olga Nayashkova 71/12, Sergey Novikov 93b (centre left), 94/2, Odua Images 91r, Tyler Olson 84/2, oriori 18b, Alexander Petrov 93tr, PictureArt 84/1, pixelrobot 68/10, Darya Prokapalo 110 (b), Elena Schweitzer 93b (centre right), somen 61/2, soupstock 36/6, spaxiax 68/6, 71/11, 74/5, Patrik Stedrak 62/3, Diana Taliun 68/9, underworld 62 (moon), verkoka 47 (Tom), vladakela 80/9, WavebreakmediaMicro 47 (Grandpa), Wisky 47 (Emma), www.1000tdw.com 110 (d), ztougas 62/1; Getty Images: Digital Vision / Rayes 30tl, iStock / Christopher Futcher 41t, KidStock 111/4, Photographer's Choice / Marcus Lyon 28 (twins), Stockbyte 28 (b); John Foxx Collection: Imagestate 62/6; MedioImages: 28 (d); Pearson Education Ltd: Studio 8 40 (d), 40 (f), 40 (l), 91l, Trevor Clifford 15l, 20, 21, 25l, 40 (a), 43tl, 49 (left), 50/1, 50/2, 50/3, 50/4, 50/5, 52, 59b, 76r, 87t, 87b, 104l, 104r, 105t, 105b, 106t, 106b, Miguel Domínguez Muñoz 47t, Tudor Photography 41/3 (right), 49 (right), 59t, Jules Selmes 40 (g), 40 (k), 41/2 (left), 41/2 (right), Rafal Trubisz 36/3, Ian Wedgewood 110 (c); Shutterstock.com: Ana Bokan 33 (a), Nina Buday 33 (c), Jacek Chabraszewski 40 (b), 41/1 (right), Coprid 80/5, Cre8tive Images 71/13, Alexander Dashewsky 68/4, 71/14, Sanjay Deva 86/4, Elenamiv 62 (sun), Elnur 80/8, 93bl, Jacek Fulawka 68/3, 74/2, Mandy Godbehear 36/7, Goodluz 28 (parents), 33 (d), gorillaimages 43 (swing), Hallgerd 40 (j), Pavel Hlystov 18c, Hariyan 61/1, iodrakon 47 (Aunt Jane), iofoto 84/4, Eric Isselee 58/3, 58/4, 58/5, Ivan Kuzmin 62/4, Maceofoto 71/6, MarcusVDT 36/1, MariusdeGraf 71/10, Rob Marmion 72/2, mexrix 71/9, Monkey Business Images 28 (c), 28 (g), Juriah Mosin 43 (swim), MShev 43tr, Maks Narodenko 71/5, Sergey Peterman 71/4, pio3 94/1, Valentina Razumova 71/3, Mikhail Rulkov 50br, shooarts 80/1, Shout It Out Design 62/2, Somchai Som 71/8, Alex Staroseltsev 68/1, StockLite 33 (b), Marek R. Swadzba 80/4, Magdalena Szachowska 43 (climb), Max Topchii 28 (f), Suzanne Tucker 43 (dance), Richard Upshur 28 (h), Kirsanov Valeriy Vladimirovich 58/1, Valentyn Volkov 68/8, 71/7, 74/1, Chamille White 80/3, Tracy Whiteside 15r, 86/3, Mark Yuill 18t; Stockdisc: 28 (grandparents); www.imagesource.com: Nigel RIches 72/3

Contents

Scope and sequence

Welcome

Vocabulary: **Time:** one o'clock, two o'clock, three o'clock, four o'clock, five o'clock, six o'clock, seven o'clock, eight o'clock, nine o'clock, ten o'clock, eleven o'clock, twelve o'clock
Daily routines: wake up, get up, eat breakfast, go to school, eat lunch, eat dinner, go to bed

Structures: What time is it? It's one o'clock.
I wake up at six o'clock.

1 My toys

Vocabulary: **Toys:** teddy bear, car, kite, doll, boat, bike, ball, truck, train
Numbers: 16–50

Structures: What's this/that? It's a bike. It's yellow.
What are these/those? They're bikes. They're yellow.
How many bikes are there? There are sixteen bikes.

Values: Friendship is important.

Cross-curricular:
Math: plus, minus, and equals

Phonics: ch, sh
chop, ship

2 My family

Vocabulary: **Family members:** grandson, uncle, aunt, granddaughter, son, daughter, cousin
Neighborhood places: house, yard, bakery, post office, restaurant, apartment

Structures: Who's he/she? He's/She's my uncle/aunt.
Where's my/your uncle? Your/My uncle is in the house.

Values: Spend time with your relatives.

Cross-curricular:
Social science: Types of family members

Phonics: th, th
this, thin

3 Move your body

Vocabulary: **Actions:** point, wave, move, nod, shake, sit down, turn around, touch
Physical abilities: jump, swim, dance, climb, swing, stand on your head, do cartwheels, do the splits

Structures: Touch your toes.
Can you jump? Yes, I can. / No, I can't
Can he/she jump? Yes, he/she can. / No, he/she can't.

Values: Exercise regularly.

Cross-curricular:
Health: Exercise actions

Phonics: ng, nk
sing, pink

4 My face

Vocabulary: **Parts of the body:** face, hair, eyes, ears, mouth, nose
Hairstyles: long, short, curly, straight, wavy, dark, blond, red, neat, messy

Structures: I have a small nose. He/She has a small nose.
Do you have a small nose? Yes, I do. / No, I don't.
Does he/she have a small nose? Yes, he/she does. / No, he/she doesn't.
He/She has long hair.
His/Her hair is long.

Values: Respect differences.

Cross-curricular:
Math: Shapes

Phonics: ai, ee
tail, sheep

5 Animals

Vocabulary: **Farm animals:** horse, sheep, cow, turkey, chicken, goat, goose, pig, duck
Wild animals: bat, crow, skunk, owl, fox

Structures: What's this/that? It has big eyes. It's black and white. It's a cow.
Is it small? Yes, it is. / No, it isn't.
Is it a bat? Yes, it is. / No, it isn't.
Are the bats big? Yes, they are. / No, they aren't.

Values: Respect animals.

Cross-curricular:
Science: Daytime and nighttime animals

Phonics: igh, oa
high, goat

6 Food

Vocabulary: **Food items:** rice, hot dogs, eggs, chicken, burgers, pizza, bananas, apples, pineapple, coconut, pumpkin, corn, toast, cereal, grapes, beans, raisins, nuts

Structures: What's your favorite food? My favorite food is pizza.
I like chicken. I don't like eggs.
He/She likes pineapple for breakfast.
He/She doesn't like pineapple for breakfast.
Does he/she like pineapple for breakfast?
Yes, he/she does. / No, he/she doesn't.

Values: Eat good food. Choose good snacks.

Cross-curricular:
Social science: Different cultures, different foods

Phonics: oo, oo
zoo, book

7 Clothes

Vocabulary: **Clothes:** dress, skirt, shoes, socks, pants, T-shirt, shirt, coat, sweater, hat, cap, boots, pajamas, jeans, sneakers, shorts

Structures: I'm wearing a white skirt.
I'm not wearing white pants.
What do you want? I want a shirt, please.
Do you want a blue shirt? Yes, I do. / No, I don't. I want a red shirt.

Values: Be polite.

Cross-curricular:
Social science: Occupations and uniforms

Phonics: ar, ir, or, ur
car, girl, corn, fur

8 Weather

Vocabulary: **Weather:** sunny, cloudy, snowy, rainy, windy, cool
Days of the week: Sunday, Monday, Tuesday, Wednesday, Thursday, Friday, Saturday
Activities: ride a bike, fly a kite, make a snowman, go for a walk, go to the beach, read a book, take a picture, watch TV

Structures: Do you like cloudy days? Yes, I do. / No, I don't.
I like cloudy days.
I don't like cloudy days.
What day is it today? It's Sunday.
What's the weather like? It's sunny.

Values: Share with friends and family.

Cross-curricular:
Science: Temperature

Phonics: ow, oy
owl, boy

Welcome

1 Listen and write. A:02

2 Listen and circle. A:03

1 Charlie

2 Rose

3 Ola

4 Uncle Dan

3 Look and match.

1 yellow

3 green

5 orange

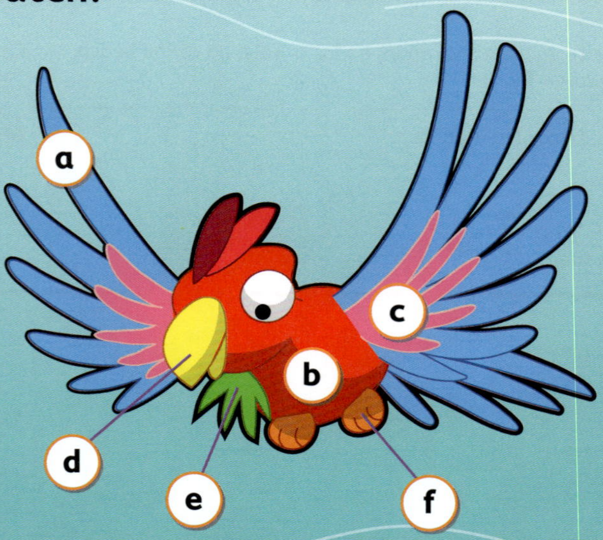

2 red

4 blue

6 pink

4 A:04 / A:05 **Listen and chant.**

Hello, Rose. How are you?
I'm fine, thank you.
And how are you?

Hello, Charlie. How are you?
I'm fine, thank you.
And how are you?

5 A:06 **Listen and number.**

6 Listen and say.

A:07

VOCABULARY

one o'clock	two o'clock	three o'clock	four o'clock	five o'clock	six o'clock

seven o'clock	eight o'clock	nine o'clock	ten o'clock	eleven o'clock	twelve o'clock

7 Listen and chant. Then draw.

A:08 / A:09

CHANT

1 What time is it? What time is it?
It's time to get up. Get out of bed!
What time is it? What time is it?
It's seven o'clock. It's seven o'clock.

2 What time is it? What time is it?
It's time to go to school, my friend!
What time is it? What time is it?
It's eight o'clock. It's eight o'clock.

3 What time is it? What time is it?
It's time to eat lunch. I want some bread!
What time is it? What time is it?
It's one o'clock. It's one o'clock.

4 What time is it? What time is it?
It's time to go to bed, sleepy head!
What time is it? What time is it?
It's ten o'clock. It's ten o'clock.

8 Listen and circle. Then ask and answer.

A:11

LOOK! A:10

What time is it?

It's one **o'clock**.

1

2

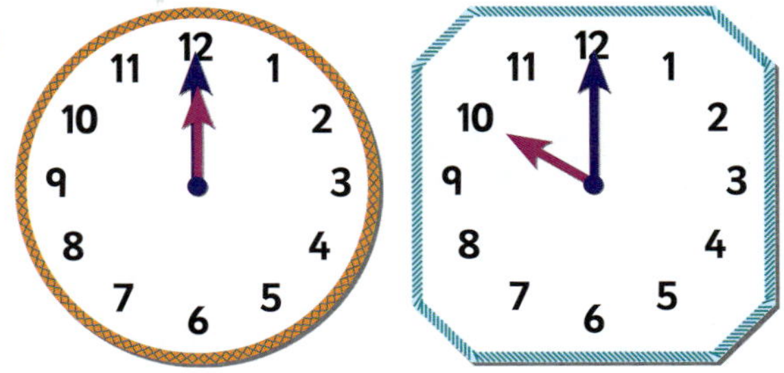

3

4

What time is it?

It's four o'clock.

9 Look and write.

1

It's ____________ o'clock.

2

It's ____________ o'clock.

3

It's ____________ o'clock.

VOCABULARY

10 Look, listen, and number.

A:12

a

wake up

b

get up

c

eat breakfast

d

go to school

e

eat lunch

f

eat dinner

g

go to bed

11 Listen and match. Then write.

A:13

1	wake up	twelve o'clock	I ______ at twelve o'clock.
2	get up	seven o'clock	I ______ at seven o'clock.
3	eat breakfast	five o'clock	I ______ at five o'clock.
4	go to school	eight o'clock	I ______ at eight o'clock.
5	eat lunch	six o'clock	I wake up at six o'clock.
6	eat dinner	nine o'clock	I ______ at nine o'clock.
7	go to bed	ten o'clock	I ______ at ten o'clock.

12 Look and write about yourself.

A:14 **LOOK!**

I **wake up at** six **o'clock**.

1 I wake up at ______________ o'clock.

2 I get up at ____________________________.

3 I eat ______________ at ____________________________.

4 I go to ______________
at ____________________________.

5 I ______________________ at ______________________.

13 Look. Listen and sing.

A:15

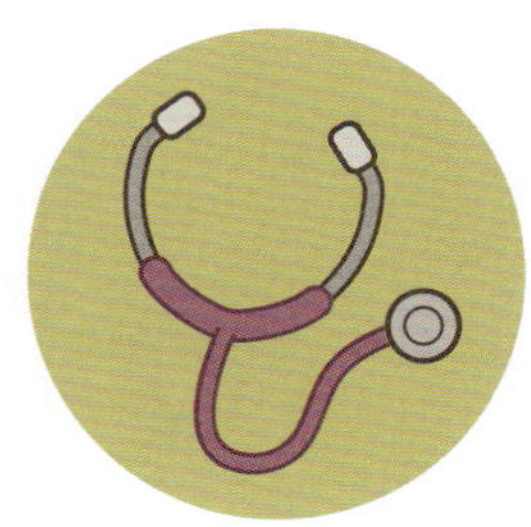

Quest A:15

1 My toys

1 What do you know?

2 A:16 Listen and find.

3 A:17 Listen and circle.

4 A:18 Listen and say.

5 Listen and chant. A:19 / A:20

What's this? It's red.
It's a car.
What's that? It's blue.
It's a boat.
What are these? They're brown.
They're teddy bears.
What are those? They're purple.
They're kites.

LOOK! A:21

What's this/that?	**It's a** bike. **It's** yellow.
What are these/those?	**They're** bikes. **They're** yellow.

6 Listen and number. Then ask and answer. A:22

these — that — this — those

What's this?

It's a ball.
It's orange.

Quest A:23

VOCABULARY

7 Listen and say. A:24

16	17	18	19
sixteen	seventeen	eighteen	nineteen
20	30	40	50
twenty	thirty	forty	fifty

SONG

8 Listen and write the number. Then sing. A:25 / A:26

Trains, trains,
How many trains?
How many trains are there?
Seventeen trains.
Seventeen trains.
I can see seventeen trains.

☐

☐

Cars, cars,
How many cars?
How many cars are there?
Fifteen cars.
Fifteen cars.
I can see fifteen cars.

Balls, balls,
How many balls?
How many balls are there?
Twenty balls.
Twenty balls.
I can see twenty balls.

☐

LOOK!

A:27

How many bikes **are there**?

There are sixteen bikes.

9 Look and circle.
Then ask and answer.

1

(nineteen / fifteen)

2

(seventeen / sixteen)

3

(twelve / twenty)

4

(fourteen / eighteen)

How many trains are there?

There are nineteen trains.

10 Look at Activity 9. Write.

WRITING

1 How many trains are there?
There are ______________________ trains.

2 How many teddy bears are there?
There are ______________________ teddy bears.

3 How many dolls are there?
There are ______________________ dolls.

4 How many trucks are there?
There are ______________________ trucks.

11 Listen to the story. Read.

A:28

STORY

12 Role-play the story.

Can understand a simple story / Can role-play a story

13 Listen. Then number in order.

a

b

c

d

VALUES

Friendship is important.

14 Look and check (✓). Then write about yourself.

1

Good friends play together and share toys.

2

Good friends listen and help.

Who is your best friend? What do you like?

_______________ is my best friend.

We like _______________,

but we don't like _______________.

MATH

15 Look and write.

1	2	3	4	5	6	7	8		10
11		13		15		17	18		20

16 Listen and stick. Then say.

A:30

Stick

\+ plus   − minus   = equals

1 [ ] +  = [ ]

2 [ ] − [ ] = 

3  + [ ] = [ ]

PROJECT

17 Draw or find pictures of toys.
Write + (plus), - (minus), and = (equals).

18 Make a math problems poster for a friend.
Give the poster a title.

HOME SCHOOL LINK

Share your math problems with your family.

PHONICS

19 A:31 Listen.

1 **chop** 2 **ship**

20 A:32 Listen and blend the sounds.

21 Circle *ch* and *sh*. Read the words aloud.

1 shell

2 chop

3 rich

4 fish

5 chin

6 ship

I CAN DO IT!

22 Listen and write the numbers.

A:33

23 Read and circle. Then say.

1 (What's this? / What are these?)
(It's a truck. / They're trucks.)

2 How many (kites / cars) are there?
There are (fifteen / twenty).

24 Look at Activity 22. Choose. Then ask and answer.

25 Listen. Then play.

A:34

What are these?

They're kites.

26 Look at Activity 25. Count and write. Then ask and answer.

How many cars are there?

There are two cars.

Now go to Poptropica English World

2 My family

1 What do you know?

2 A:35 Listen and find.

3 A:36 Listen and circle.

4 A:37 Listen and say.

5 Listen and chant.

A:38 / A:39

Who's he? He's my grandpa.
Who's she? She's my aunt.
Who's he? He's my uncle.
Who's she? She's Ola!
Who are they? They're my cousins.
They're my family. Hey, hey!

LOOK!

A:40

Who's he/she? He's/She's my uncle/aunt.

Who's = Who is

6 Listen and number. Then repeat.

A:41

a  ☐

b  ☐

c  ☐

Quest A:42

VOCABULARY

7 A:43 Stick. Then listen and say.

1 
house

2 
yard

3 

bakery

4 

post office

5 

restaurant

6 
apartment

Stick

SONG

8 A:44 / A:45 Listen and match. Then sing.

Where's my grandma? Where's my grandma?
She's in the house. Snore, snore, snore.
Where's my grandma? Where's my grandma?
She's in the house. Snore, snore, snore.

Where's my cousin? Where's my cousin?
He's in the yard. Play, play, play.
Where's my cousin? Where's my cousin?
He's in the yard. Play, play, play.

Where's my daughter? Where's my daughter?
She's in the bakery. Buy, buy, buy.
Where's my daughter? Where's my daughter?
She's in the bakery. Buy, buy, buy.

Where's my uncle? Where's my uncle?
He's in the restaurant. Eat, eat, eat.
Where's my uncle? Where's my uncle?
He's in the restaurant. Eat, eat, eat.

a 

b 

c 

d 

9 Listen and match. Then ask and answer.

A:47

LOOK! A:46

Where's my uncle?	**Your** uncle **is in the** house.
Where's your uncle?	**My** uncle **is in the** house.

1 Where's my mom?

2 Where's my grandma?

3 Where's my uncle?

4 Where's my aunt?

5 Where's my grandson?

6 Where's my cousin?

Where's my mom?

Your mom is in the house.

SPEAKING

10 Complete for yourself. Then ask a friend.

aunt cousin grandma uncle

	Post office	Restaurant	Bakery	House
me				
my friend				

Where's your grandma?

My grandma is in the post office.

STORY

11 Listen to the story. Read.

A:48

12 Role-play the story.

13 Read and write.

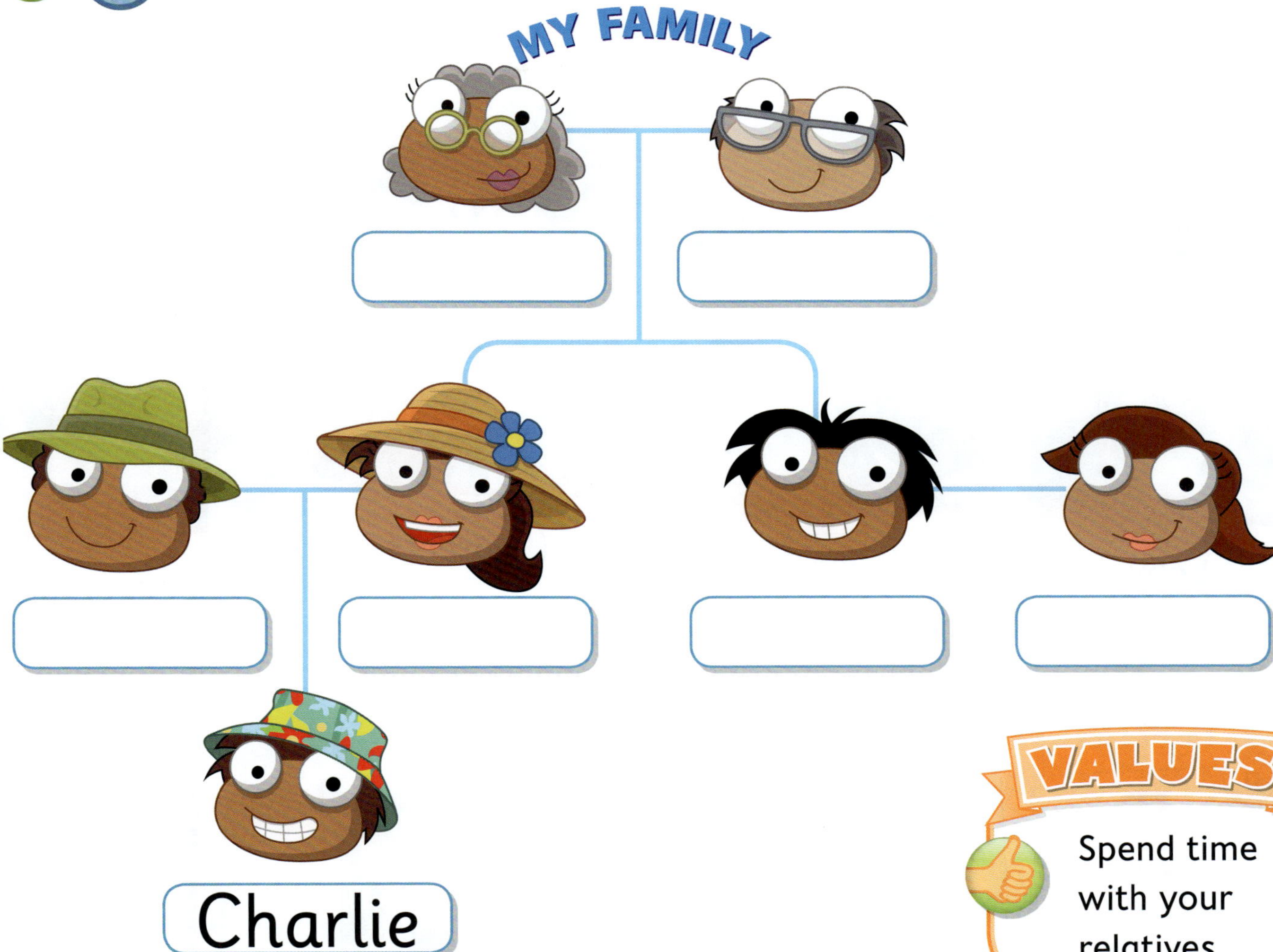

VALUES

Spend time with your relatives.

14 Read and write. Then draw your relatives.

How many aunts do you have?

____

How many uncles do you have?

____

How many cousins do you have?

____

SOCIAL SCIENCE

15 Listen and point. Then say.

A:49

young

old

baby

twins

parents

grandparents

16 Look and match.

a

b

c

d

1 twins

2 parents

3 babies

4 grandparents

e

f

g

h

PROJECT

17 Draw pictures of your family.
Label the pictures.

18 Make a poster about your family. Give the poster a title.

HOME SCHOOL LINK

Display your poster at home.

PHONICS

19 A:50 Listen.

1 **this** 2 **thin**

20 A:51 Listen and blend the sounds.

21 Circle *th*. Read the words aloud.

1 math 2 this 3 that 4 path 5 thick 6 thin

I CAN DO IT!

22 A:52 **Listen and check (✓). Ask a friend.**

23 **Draw a relative.**
Then write and say.

Where's your ________?
My ________ is in the
________________.

24 **Choose. Then ask and answer.**

Where's your sister?

My sister's in the bakery.

HAVE FUN

25 Ask and answer.

26 Look at Activity 25. Then write.

1 Where's your mom? My mom is in the ______________.

2 Where's your dad? My dad is in the ______________.

3 Where's your grandma? My grandma is in the ______________.

4 Where's your grandpa? My grandpa is in the ______________.

Now go to Poptropica English World

Review Units 1 and 2

1 **Listen and draw. Then write.** A:53

1  I wake up at ________ o'clock.

2  I go to school at ________ o'clock.

3  I eat dinner at ________ o'clock.

2 **Read and circle. Then write.**

1 

What's (this / that)?
It's a ________.

2 

What are (these / those)?
They're ________.

3 

What are (these / those)?
They're ________.

4 

What's (this / that)?
It's a ________.

3 **Write.**

1 s ____ n 2 n ___ t ___ 3 t ____ y 4 f ____

Can talk about my toys

4 A:54 Listen and number.

5 A:55 Write. Then listen and match.

a __________ b __________ c __________ d __________

3 Move your body

1 What do you know?

2 A:56 Listen and find.

3 A:57 Listen and circle.

4 A:58 Listen and say.

5 A:59 / A:60 **Listen and chant.**

Arms, arms, wave your arms,
Wave your arms with me.

Toes, toes, touch your toes,
Touch your toes with me.

Nod, nod, nod your head,
Nod your head with me.

Legs, legs, move your legs,
Move your legs with me.

Turn around.
Move, wave, shake.
And sit down!

A:61 **LOOK!**

Touch your toes.

6 A:62 **Listen and number. Then say.**

Quest A:63

7 Listen and do. Then say.

A:64

VOCABULARY

1

jump

2

swim

3

dance

4

climb

5

swing

6

stand on your head

7

do cartwheels

8

do the splits

8 Listen and ✓ or ✗. Then sing.

A:65 / A:66

SONG

Can you jump?
Yes, I can.
Can you jump?
Yes, I can.
Can you jump?
Yes, I can.
I can jump! Hooray!

Can you swim?
Yes, I can.
Can you swim?
Yes, I can.
Can you swim?
Yes, I can.
I can swim! Hooray!

Can you climb?
No, I can't.
Can you climb?
No, I can't.
Can you climb?
No, I can't.
I can't climb. Boo hoo!

Can you dance?
No, I can't.
Can you dance?
No, I can't.
Can you dance?
No, I can't.
I can't dance. Boo hoo!

I can...

jump. ☐ climb. ☐ swim. ☐ dance. ☐

LOOK!

A:67

Can you jump?	Yes, **I can**. / No, **I can't**.
Can he/she jump?	Yes, **he/she can**. / No, **he/she can't**.

9 **Look, read, and circle. Then ask and answer.**

1 Can you do cartwheels?

(Yes, I can. / No, I can't.)

2 Can you do the splits?

(Yes, I can. / No, I can't.)

3 Can you swim?

(Yes, I can. / No, I can't.)

Can he do cartwheels?

Yes, he can.

10 **Complete for yourself. Then ask a friend.** WRITING

	do cartwheels	do the splits	stand on your head	swing	swim
me					
my friend					

11 **Write about yourself and a friend.**

I can ________________. I can't ________________.

My friend can ________________.

He/She can't ________________.

12 Listen to the story. Read.

STORY

13 Role-play the story.

Can understand a simple story / Can role-play a story

14 Read and number. Then match.

a

Jump! Touch your toes! ☐

b

Swing! Do the splits! Move your body! ☐

c

Move your feet! Stand on your head! ☐

d

Stand on one leg! Turn around! ☐

or

VALUES

Exercise regularly.

15 Look and stick.

EXERCISE

NOT EXERCISE

Stick

HEALTH

16 Listen and number. Then say.

A:69

a

pull

b

push

c

hop

d

jump rope

17 Listen and number. Then move.

A:70

a

Clap your hands.

b

Jump.

c

Stamp your feet.

d

Wave your arms.

e

Move your head.

f

Dance.

g

Touch your toes.

h

Shake your body.

i

Pull.

j

Push.

k

Hop.

l

Jump rope.

PROJECT

18 Work in small groups. Choose some actions to make an exercise routine.

19 A:71 Listen. Then show the class an exercise routine.

1

2

3

4

HOME SCHOOL LINK

Share your exercise routine with your family.

PHONICS

20 A:72 Listen.

1 sing   2 pink

21 A:73 Listen and blend the sounds.

22 Circle *ng* and *nk*. Read the words aloud.

1 pink

2 sing

3 long

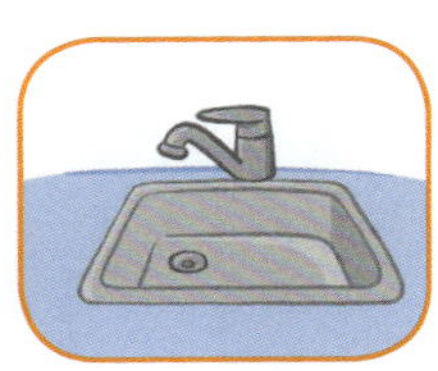
4 sink

5 ring

6 ink

I CAN DO IT!

23 Listen and number. Ask a friend.

24 What can you do? Draw. Then write and say.

I can ______________________.

I can't ____________________.

25 Listen and check (✓).

1
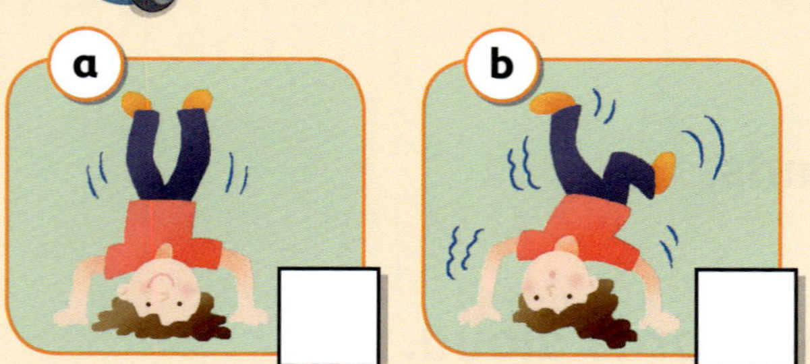

2

3

4
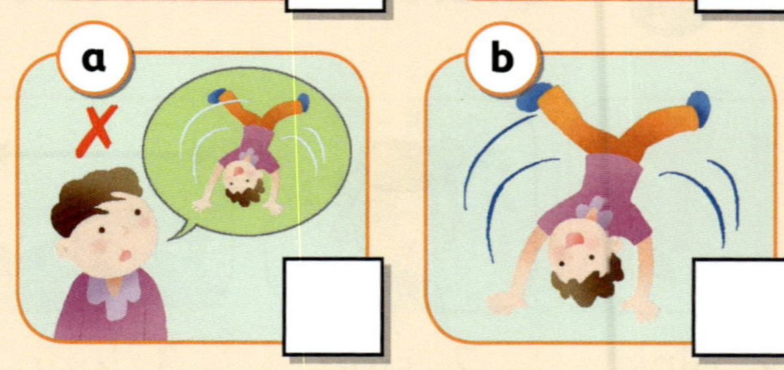

26 Choose and say. Then do.

wave

touch

point

move

shake

27 Ask a friend and check (✓). Then say.

Now go to Poptropica English World

4 My face

1 What do you know?

2 B:02 Listen and find.

3 B:03 Listen and circle.

4 B:04 Listen and say.

Can identify parts of the face

5 Listen and chant.

B:05 / B:06

Do you have small eyes?
No, I don't.

Do you have big eyes?
Yes, I do!

Does he have short hair?
No, he doesn't.

Does he have long hair?
Yes, he does!

Does she have a big nose?
No, she doesn't.

Does she have a small nose?
Yes, she does!

LOOK!

B:07

I have a small nose.	**He**/**She has** a small nose.
Do you have a small nose?	Yes, **I do**. / No, **I don't**.
Does he/**she have** a small nose?	Yes, **he**/**she does**. / No, **he**/**she doesn't**.

6 Listen and draw. Then draw yourself and say.

B:08

Quest B:09

7 Stick. Then listen and say.

B:10

VOCABULARY

1 
long

2 
short

3 
curly

4 
straight

5 
wavy

6 
dark

7 
blond

8 
red

9 
neat

10 
messy

Stick

8 Listen and number. Then sing.

B:11 / B:12

SONG

1 Who is it? Who can it be?
Who is it? Listen to me!
She has blue eyes, blue eyes,
And a small nose, a small nose.
She has small ears, small ears,
And long, straight hair.
Who is it? It's Susie!

2 Who is it? Who can it be?
Who is it? Listen to me!
He has brown eyes, brown eyes,
And a small nose, a small nose,
He has a big mouth, a big mouth,
And short, curly hair.
Who is it? It's Tommy.

3 Who is it? Who can it be?
Who is it? Listen to me!
She has green eyes, green eyes,
And a big nose, a big nose.
She has big ears, big ears,
And neat, blond hair.
Who is it? It's Mary!

a  ☐

b  ☐

c  ☐

4

9 Listen and number. Then say.

a

b

c

d

LOOK!

He/**She has** long hair.

His/**Her** hair **is** long.

He has blond hair.
His hair is messy.

10 Look, write, and circle.

WRITING

Grandpa

Emma

Tom

Aunt Jane

1 Who is it?
It's ___________. (His / Her) hair is straight and blond.

2 Who is it?
It's ___________. (His / Her) hair is dark and curly.

3 Who is it?
It's ___________. (His / Her) hair is short and curly.

4 Who is it?
It's ___________. (His / Her) hair is short and straight.

STORY

11 Listen to the story. Read.

12 Role-play the story.

13 Read and circle. Then check (✓).

1 Does Tim have long hair? (Yes, he does. / No, he doesn't.)

2 Does Tim have short hair? (Yes, he does. / No, he doesn't.)

3 Does Tim have messy hair? (Yes, he does. / No, he doesn't.)

4 Does Tim have glasses? (Yes, he does. / No, he doesn't.)

a  ☐

b  ☐

c  ☐

d  ☐

14 Complete for yourself. Then ask a friend.

me				
my friend				

VALUES

Respect differences.

15 Write about yourself.

I have ________________.
Do you have curly hair?

Yes, I do.

MATH

16 B:16 Listen and point. Then say.

17 Count and write.

_________ circles

_______ triangle

_______ squares

_______ rectangles

_______ triangles

_______ squares

_______ rectangles

_______ circle

PROJECT

18 Draw shapes in different sizes.
Color the shapes different colors.

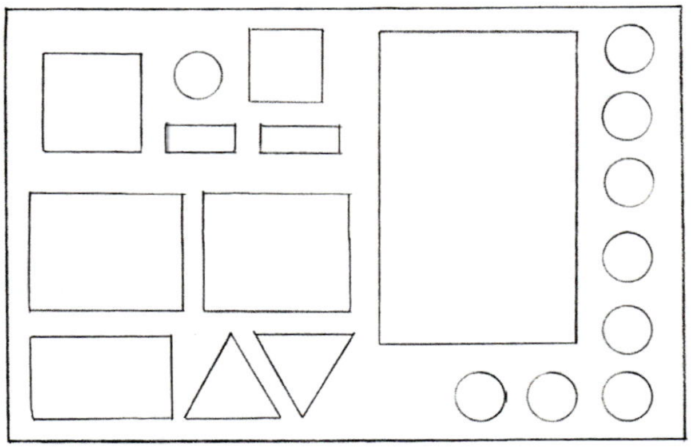

19 Cut out the shapes. Make a picture with shapes.

HOME SCHOOL LINK

Make another picture with shapes at home.

PHONICS

20 B:17 Listen.

1 tail   2 sheep

21 B:18 Listen and blend the sounds.

22 Circle *ai* and *ee*. Read the words aloud.

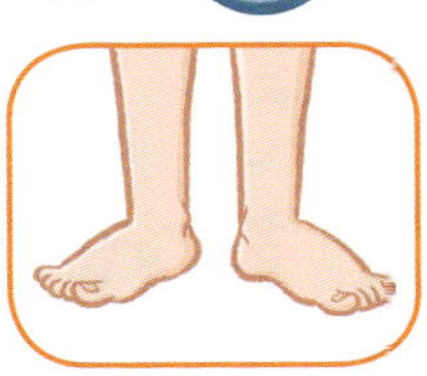
1 feet

2 rain

3 mail

4 sheep

5 tail

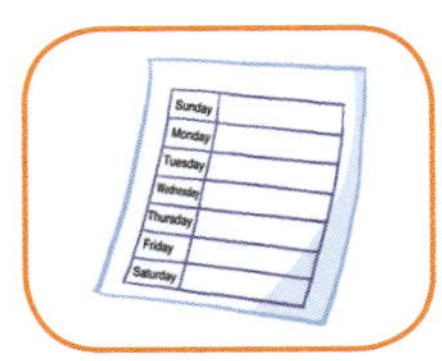
6 week

I CAN DO IT!

23 Listen and check (✓).

B:19

24 Draw a friend. Then write.

This is __________.
(He / She) has _________ eyes,
_________ hair, a _________
nose, and a __________ mouth.

25 Choose from Activity 23. Then ask and answer.

26 Draw. Then circle and write.

(He / She) has __________ eyes.

(He / She) has a __________ mouth.

(He / She) has __________ ears.

(He / She) has a __________ nose.

(He / She) has __________ hair. (long/short)

(He / She) has __________ hair. (color)

(He / She) has __________ hair. (wavy/curly/straight)

27 Ask, answer, and check (✓). Then draw.

Does she have big eyes?

Yes, she does.

eyes	☐	big	☐	small		
mouth	☐	big	☐	small		
ears	☐	big	☐	small		
nose	☐	big	☐	small		
hair	☐	long	☐	short		
	☐	straight	☐	curly	☐	wavy
	☐	dark	☐	blond	☐	red

Now go to Poptropica English World

Review Units 3 and 4

1 Listen and check (✓).

1
a 
b 

2
a 
b 

3
a 
b 

4
a 
b 

5
a 
b 

6
a 
b 

2 Write.

1

She can ____________ ____________.

2

He ____________ ____________.

3

He ____________ ____________.

4

She ____________ ____________.

5

He ____________ ____________.

6

She ____________ ____________.

Can talk about body movements and actions

3 B:21 Listen and draw.

1

boy

2

girl

4 B:22 Listen and write.

Simon

Ann

Bob

Sally

1 Who is it? It's ____________________.

2 Who is it? It's ____________________.

3 Who is it? It's ____________________.

4 Who is it? It's ____________________.

5 Who is it? It's ____________________.

5 Animals

1 What do you know?

2 B:23 Listen and find.

3 B:24 Listen and circle.

4 B:25 Listen and say.

Can identify farm animals

5 B:26/B:27 **Listen and chant.**

What's this? What's this?
It has a big nose.
It's big and gray.
It's a horse! Yes!

What are these? What are these?
They have two legs.
They're small and brown.
They're chickens! Yes!

B:28 **LOOK!**

What's this/that?	**It has** big eyes. **It's** black and white. **It's** a cow.

6 B:29 **Listen and number. Then ask and answer.**

a  ☐

b  ☐

c  ☐

d  ☐

What's this?
It has long legs.
It's black and white.

It's a cow.

Quest B:30

7 Stick. Then listen and say.

B:31

VOCABULARY

1 
bat

2 
crow

3 
skunk

4 
owl

5 
fox

TIP!
one fox
two foxes

Stick

8 Listen and match. Then sing.

B:32 / B:33

SONG

Chorus:

I'm Max. And I'm Maisie.
We're animal crazy!

1 What's this?
What's this?
It's small and green.
It has big eyes.
It's a frog!

(Chorus)

2 What are these?
What are these?
They're black and white.
They have a tail.
They're skunks!

(Chorus)

3 What's that?
What's that?
It's small and gray.
It has two wings.
It's a bat!

(Chorus)

4 What are those?
What are those?
They're thin and black.
They have two legs.
They're crows!

(Chorus)

a 

b 

c 

d 

LOOK!

B:34

Is it small? **Is it** a bat?	Yes, **it is**. / No, **it isn't**.
Are the bats big?	Yes, **they are**. / No, **they aren't**.

9 B:35 **Listen and circle. Then ask and answer.**

1

(Yes, it is. /
Yes, they are.)

2

(No, it isn't. /
No, they aren't.)

3

(No, it isn't. /
Yes, it is.)

4

(Yes, they are. /
No, they aren't.)

SPEAKING

10 **Choose. Then ask and answer.**

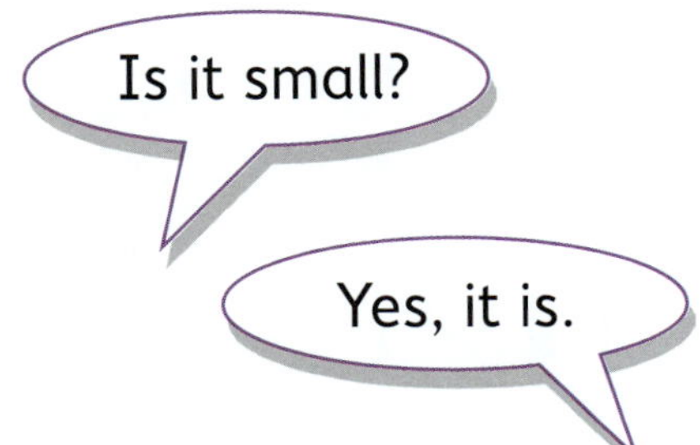

11 Listen to the story. Read.

STORY

12 Role-play the story.

Can understand a simple story / Can role-play a story

13 Read and circle.

1 

Are cows big?
(Yes, they are. / No, they aren't.)

2 

Is that a sheep?
(Yes, it is. / No, it isn't. It's a goat.)

3 

Are these turkeys?
(Yes, they are. / No, they aren't. They're chickens.)

4 

Are horses VERY big?
(Yes, they are. / No, they aren't.)

VALUES

Respect animals.

14 Show how animals help us. Look and stick.

1 

2 

3 

4 

Stick

SCIENCE

15 Listen and point. Then say.

B:37

16 Read and find. Then write.

1. It's brown.
   It's awake at night.
   It's a ____________.

2. It has two legs and a big head.
   It's asleep in the day.
   It's an ____________.

3. It's black and white.
   It's awake in the day.
   It's a ____________.

4. It has two legs.
   It's asleep at night.
   It's a ____________.

PROJECT

17 Draw or find pictures of different animals. Label the pictures.

18 Make a poster about animals. Give your poster a title.

HOME SCHOOL LINK

Share your poster with your family.

PHONICS

19 B:38 Listen.

1 **high** 2 **goat**

20 B:39 Listen and blend the sounds.

21 Circle *igh* and *oa*. Read the words aloud.

1 boat

2 high

3 goat

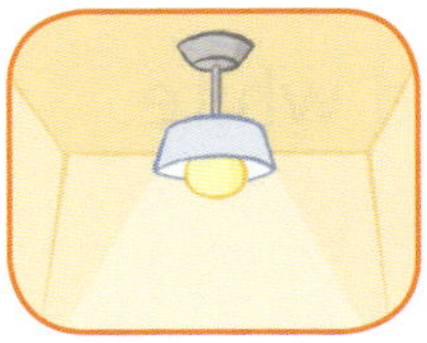
4 light

5 soap

6 coat

I CAN DO IT!

22 B:40 **Listen and number. Ask a friend.**

a 

b 

c 

d 

23 **Draw an animal. Then ask and answer.**

Is it big?

Is it thin?

24 **Read and match. Then write.**

1 It's fat. It has four legs.

2 It's big. It's gray.
It has four legs.

3 It has short legs.
It has wings.

4 It's big. It's black and white.
It's fat.

a 

b 

c 

d 

25 Circle the one that doesn't belong. Say.

1

2

3

4

5

Now go to Poptropica English World

6 Food

1 What do you know?

2 B:41 Listen and find.

3 B:42 Listen and circle.

4 B:43 Listen and say.

Can identify food items

5 Listen and chant.

B:44 / B:45

I like chicken. I like rice.
I don't like fish. I don't like pizza.

I like eggs. I like apples.
I don't like bananas. I don't like burgers.

What's your favorite food?
My favorite food is hot dogs!

LOOK!

B:46

What's your favorite food?	**My favorite food is** pizza.
I like chicken.	**I don't like** eggs.

6 Look and write. Then draw and say.

1

I like ____________.

2

I don't like ____________.

3

I don't like ____________.

4

I like ____________.

My favorite food

I like ____________
____________.

Quest B:47

7 Listen and say.

B:48

VOCABULARY

1 
pineapple

2 
coconut

3 
pumpkin

4 
corn

5 
toast

6 
cereal

7 
grapes

8 
beans

9 
raisins

10 
nuts

8 Listen and circle. Then sing.

B:49 / B:50

SONG

I eat breakfast, I eat lunch, I eat dinner. How about you?
I eat breakfast, I eat lunch, I eat dinner. How about you?

I like  /  and  / , too.
I like  / . How about you?
I like  / . My favorite dish!
But I don't like  / !

(Chorus)

I like  /  and  / , too.
I like  / . How about you?
I like  / . It's very nice.
But I don't like  / !

(Chorus)

LOOK!

B:51

He/She	likes / doesn't like	pineapple for breakfast.
Does he/she like pineapple for breakfast?		Yes, he/she does. / No, he/she doesn't.

9 **Look and circle. Then ask and answer.**

1

She (likes / doesn't like) toast for breakfast.

2

Does he like grapes for breakfast?
(Yes, he does. / No, he doesn't.)

3

Does he like corn for lunch?
(Yes, he does. / No, he doesn't.)

Does she like toast for breakfast?

Yes, she does.

10 B:52 **Listen and stick. Then say.**

SPEAKING

1

2

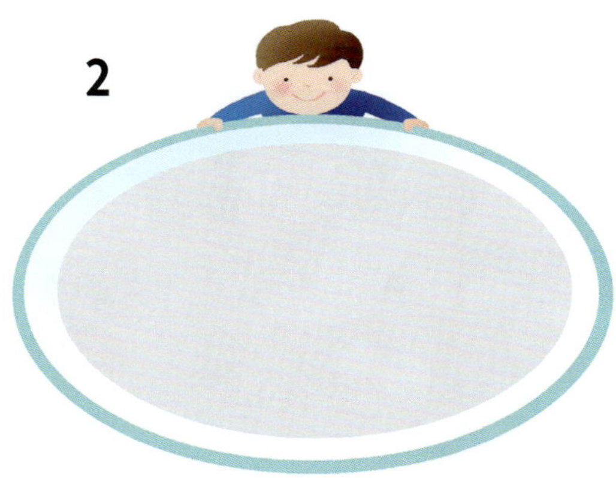

She likes cereal for breakfast.

I like toast and grapes for breakfast.

Stick

11 B:53 Listen to the story. Read.

STORY

12 Role-play the story.

13 Read and check (✓).

		YES	NO
1	Charlie likes apple juice.		
2	Rose doesn't like apples.		
3	Uncle Dan likes pineapple for lunch.		
4	Ola likes banana milkshakes.		
5	Charlie's favorite cake is chocolate cake.		
6	Uncle Dan likes chicken and rice for dinner.		
7	Rose likes milk.		
8	Charlie likes salad for dinner.		

14 Look and circle the good food and snacks.

VALUES

Eat good food. Choose good snacks.

SOCIAL SCIENCE

15 Read, look, and match. Then say.

1

2

3

a I like eggs, tortillas, and juice for breakfast.

b I like noodles, vegetables, and tea for breakfast.

c I like croissants, yogurt, and coffee for breakfast.

16 Complete for yourself. Then ask a friend and write.

What's your favorite food?

I like chicken and salad for dinner.

	NAME	DINNER
1	Me	
2	Friend	chicken and salad
3		
4		
5		

17 Show and tell a friend.

My friend likes chicken and salad for dinner.

PROJECT

18 Draw or find pictures of your favorite lunch or dinner. Label the pictures.

19 Make a poster of your favorite lunch or dinner. Give your poster a title.

HOME SCHOOL LINK

Help to make your favorite meal at home.

PHONICS

20 B:54 Listen.

1 zoo   2 book

21 B:55 Listen and blend the sounds.

22 Underline *oo*. Read the words aloud.

1 moon

2 cook

3 zoo

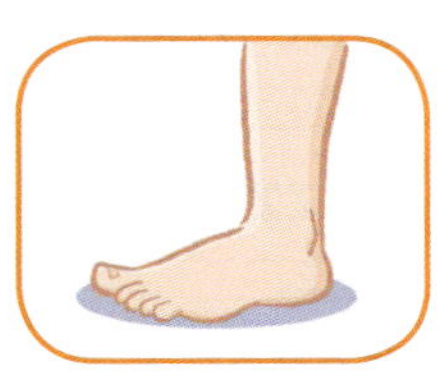
4 foot

5 book

6 food

I CAN DO IT!

23 Look and write. Ask a friend.

1  ____________

2  ____________

3  ____________

4  ____________

5  ____________

What's your favorite food?

Do you like pumpkin?

24 Listen and check (✓).

B:56

1 a 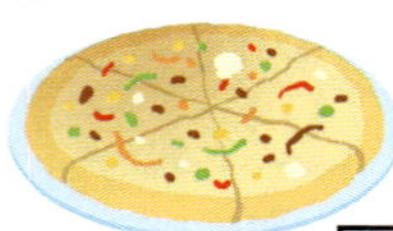 ☐ b  ☐

2 a  ☐ b  ☐

3 a  ☐ b  ☐

4 a  ☐ b  ☐

25 Ask a friend and circle. Then draw.

Do you like beans for lunch?

No, I don't.

burgers grapes

chicken nuts

hot dogs apples

pizza pumpkin

beans corn

HAVE FUN

26 **Play the game.**

27 **Write. Then ask and answer.**

1 I like __________ and __________ for breakfast.

2 I like __________ and __________ for dinner.

28 **Write.**

1 My friend likes __________ and __________ for breakfast.

2 My friend likes __________ and __________ for dinner.

Now go to Poptropica English World

Review Units 5 and 6

1 Ask and answer.

2 Write.

1

It's a ______________.

It's ______________.

It has ______________.

2

It's an ______________.

It's ______________.

It has ______________.

3

It's a ______________.

It's ______________.

It has ______________.

Can talk about animals

3 B:57 Listen and number. Then say for you.

a

b

c

d

I like eggs and toast, but I don't like yogurt.

I like eggs, toast, and bananas.

4 B:58 Listen and circle.

1

2

7 Clothes

1 What do you know?

2 B:59 Listen and find.

3 B:60 Listen and circle.

4 B:61 Listen and say.

Can identify clothes

5 Listen and chant. B:62/B:63

I'm wearing a purple skirt,
A purple skirt, a purple skirt.
I'm wearing a purple skirt.
How about you?

I'm not wearing green shoes,
Green shoes, green shoes.
I'm not wearing green shoes.
They're brown, brown, brown.

I'm not wearing pink socks,
Pink socks, pink socks.
I'm wearing white socks.
How about you?

LOOK! B:64

I'm wearing a white skirt.

I'm not wearing white pants.

6 Listen and color. Then say. B:65

I'm wearing a yellow dress and red shoes.

Quest B:66

7 Listen and say.

VOCABULARY

1 
shirt

2 
coat

3 
sweater

4 
hat

5 
cap

6 
boots

7 
pajamas

8 
jeans

9 
sneakers

10 
shorts

8 Listen and number. Then sing.

SONG

1 Good morning!
Good morning!
Take off your pajamas.
It's time for school.

2 Put on your shirt.
Put on your jeans.
Put on your sneakers.
Off you go!
It's time for school.

3 Good night!
Good night!
Put on your pajamas.
It's time for bed.

4 Take off your hat.
Take off your sweater.
Take off your boots.
Off you go! It's time for bed.
Good night! Good night!
Good night! Good night!

a 

b 

c 

d 

LOOK!

B:70

What do you want?	I want a shirt, please.
Do you want a blue shirt?	Yes, I do. / No, I don't. I want a red shirt.

9 Listen and circle. Then ask and answer.

B:71

1 

2 

3 

What do you want?

I want boots, please.

Do you want brown boots?

No, I don't. I want red boots, please.

10 Listen and stick. Then ask and answer.

B:72

LISTENING

I want...	I don't want...

Do you want a black T-shirt?

No, I don't. I want a white T-shirt.

Stick

11 B:73 Listen to the story. Read.

STORY

12 Role-play the story.

Can understand a simple story / Can role-play a story

13 Read, look, and match.

1 I'm wearing pants. Where's my dress?

2 Do you want this pink dress?

3 Where's my hat? Do you have my hat?

4 These are for you.

VALUES

Be polite.

14 Look and stick.

Stick

SOCIAL SCIENCE

15 Listen and read. Then say.

B:74

1

I'm a firefighter.
I'm wearing a helmet.

firefighter

2

I'm a chef. I'm
wearing a white hat.

chef

3

I'm a nurse. I'm
wearing a white dress.

nurse

4

I'm a police officer.
I'm wearing a badge.

police officer

16 Listen and number.

B:75

a

☐

b

☐

c

☐

d

☐

PROJECT

17 Draw a picture of someone wearing a uniform. Label the clothes.

18 Make a poster describing a uniform. Give your poster a title.

HOME SCHOOL LINK

Draw a picture of your favorite clothes. Share with your family.

PHONICS

19 B:76 Listen.

1 **car** 2 **girl** 3 **corn** 4 **fur**

20 B:77 Listen and blend the sounds.

21 Underline *ar, ir, or,* and *ur*. Read the words aloud.

1 shark

2 corn

3 girl

4 surf

5 car

6 fur

I CAN DO IT!

22 Listen and match.

B:78

1 2 3 4

a b c d

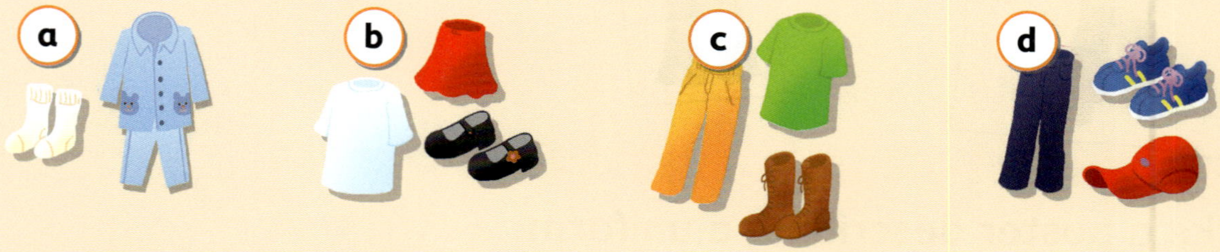

23 Draw and color your clothes. Then write.

I'm wearing ____________________

____

________________________________.

24 Listen and check (✓).

B:79

1

a  ☐

b  ☐

2

a  ☐

b  ☐

3

a  ☐

b  ☐

4

a  ☐

b  ☐

25 Color and say.

26 Look and write.

I want ____________________

____

____________________________.

Now go to Poptropica English World

8 Weather

1 What do you know?

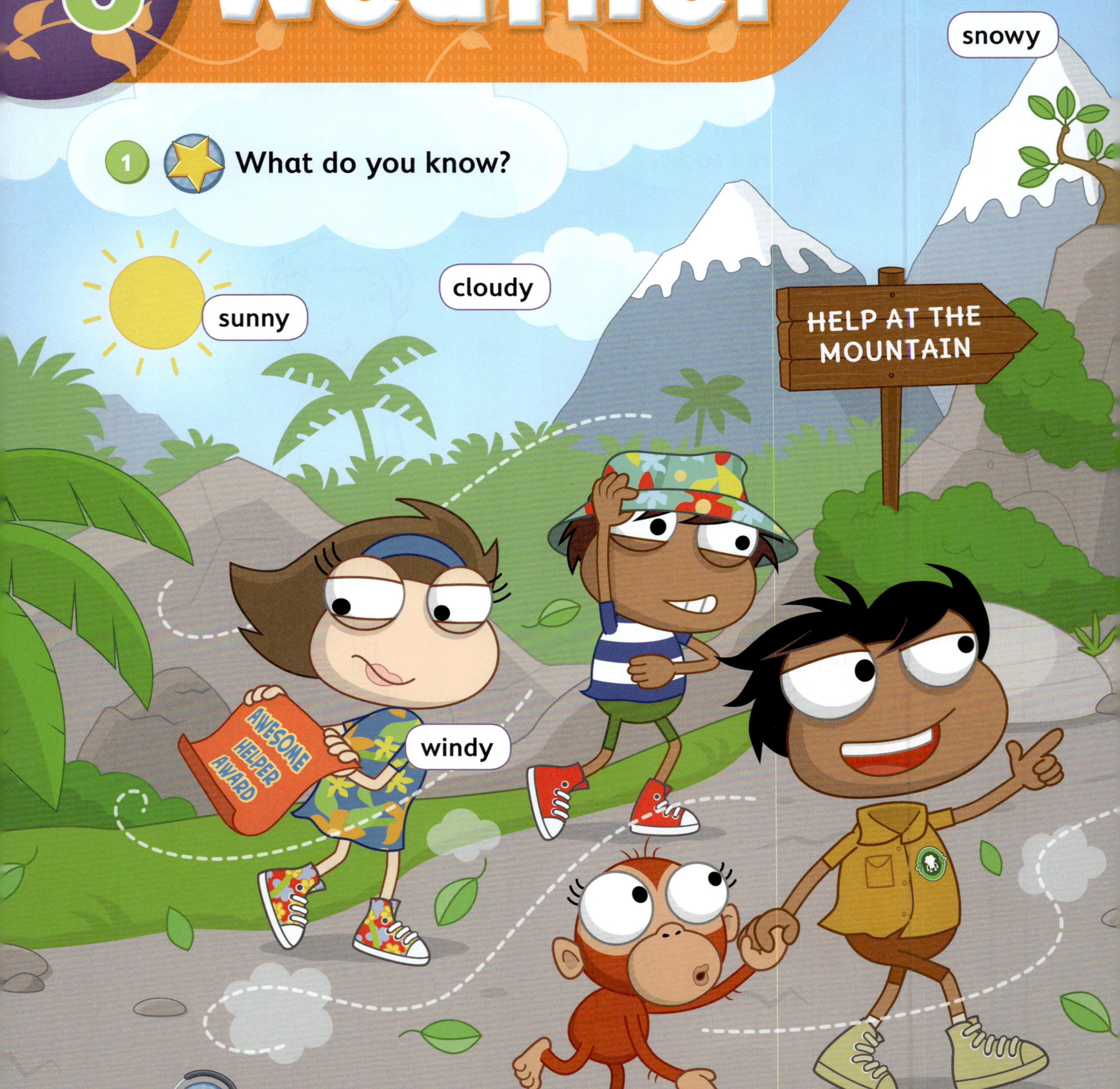

2 C:02 Listen and find.

3 C:03 Listen and circle.

4 C:04 Listen and say.

5 Listen and chant.

C:05 / C:06

Do you like sunny days?
Sunny days, sunny days?
Do you like sunny days?
Yes, I do!

Do you like rainy days?
Rainy days, rainy days?
Do you like rainy days?
No, I don't!

Do you like snowy days?
Snowy days, snowy days?
Do you like snowy days?
Yes, I do!

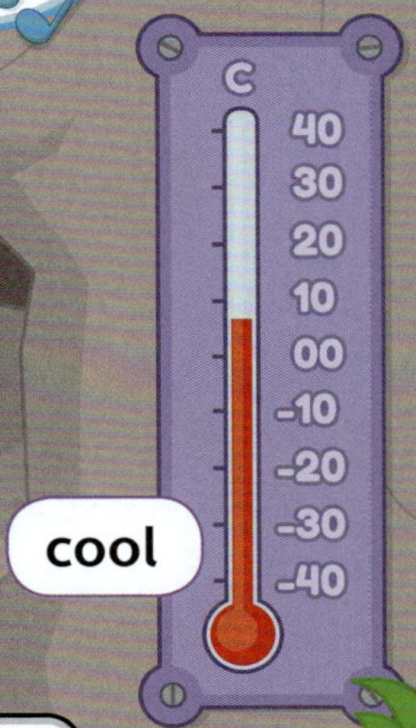

LOOK!

C:07

Do you like cloudy days?	Yes, **I do**. / No, **I don't**.
I like cloudy days.	**I don't like** cloudy days.

6 Listen and draw. Then say.

C:08

Quest C:09

VOCABULARY

7 Listen and say.

1 

ride a bike

2 

fly a kite

3 

make a snowman

4 

go for a walk

5 

go to the beach

6 

read a book

7 

take a picture

8 

watch TV

SONG

8 Listen and number. Then sing.

1 What day is it today?
It's Monday. Monday!
What's the weather like?
It's sunny. It's sunny.
Let's go for a walk!

2 What day is it today?
It's Friday. Friday!
What's the weather like?
It's snowy. It's snowy.
Let's make a snowman!

3 What day is it today?
It's Wednesday. Wednesday!
What's the weather like?
It's windy. It's windy.
Let's fly a kite.

I like sunny days,
I like windy days.
I like snowy days,
Let's have fun and play.

a 

b 

c 

Can identify activities for different types of weather

LOOK!

C:13

What day is it today?	It's Sunday.
What's the weather like?	It's sunny.

9 C:14 **Listen, circle, and draw. Then ask and answer.**

1
Sunday Monday Tuesday
Wednesday Thursday
Friday Saturday

It's windy.
It's cool.
It's sunny.

2
Sunday Monday Tuesday
Wednesday Thursday
Friday Saturday

It's cloudy.
It's sunny.
It's windy.

3
Sunday Monday Tuesday
Wednesday Thursday
Friday Saturday

It's snowy.
It's rainy.
It's cool.

10 **Write about yourself.** WRITING

What day is it today? ______________________________

What's the weather like? ______________________________

Do you like ______________ days? (Yes / No), I ______________.

STORY

11 C:15 Listen to the story. Read.

12 Role-play the story.

13 Number the pictures in order. Then write.

It's ______________________.

It's ______________________.

It's ______________________.

It's ______________________.

14 Circle what you can share.

VALUES

Share with friends and family.

15 C:16 **Listen and point. Then write and say.**

SCIENCE

1

freezing

2

cold

3

warm

4

hot

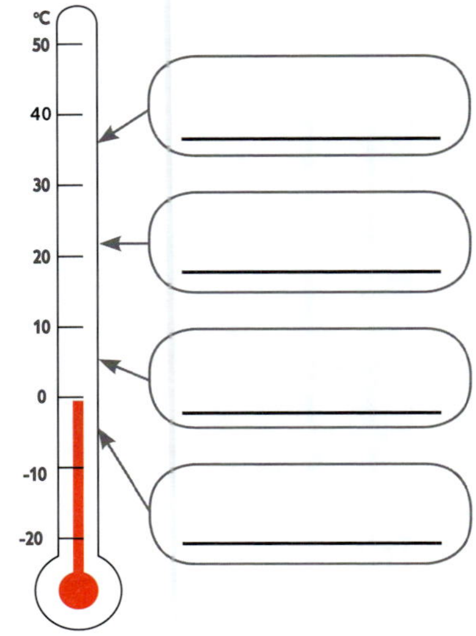

16 C:17 **Listen. Then write.**

1

It's sunny.
It's ______________.
Let's ________________.

2

It's windy.
It's ______________.
Let's ________________.

3

It's cloudy.
It's ______________.
Let's ________________.

4

It's snowy.
It's ______________.
Let's ________________.

5

It's rainy.
It's ______________.
Let's ________________.

PROJECT

17 Draw pictures of weather conditions. Color the pictures.

18 Make a weather chart. Write the days of the week.

HOME SCHOOL LINK

Take your weather chart home and complete for every day of the week.

PHONICS

19 C:18 Listen.

1 **owl** 2 **boy**

20 C:19 Listen and blend the sounds.

21 Underline *ow* and *oy*. Read the words aloud.

1 boy

2 owl

3 toy

4 cow

5 cowboy

6 down

I CAN DO IT!

22 Write. Then listen and number.

C:20

1 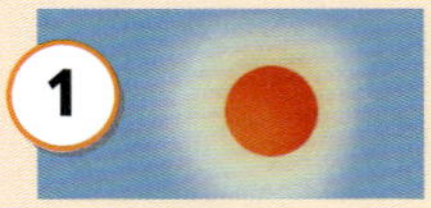
It's
____________.

2 
It's
____________.

3 
It's
____________.

4 
It's
____________.

5 
It's
____________.

Monday	Tuesday	Wednesday	Thursday	Friday

23 Draw yourself on your favorite day. Then write.

It's ____________________.

It's ____________________.

I like ________________ days.

Let's ____________________.

24 Listen and check (✓).

C:21

1 a  b 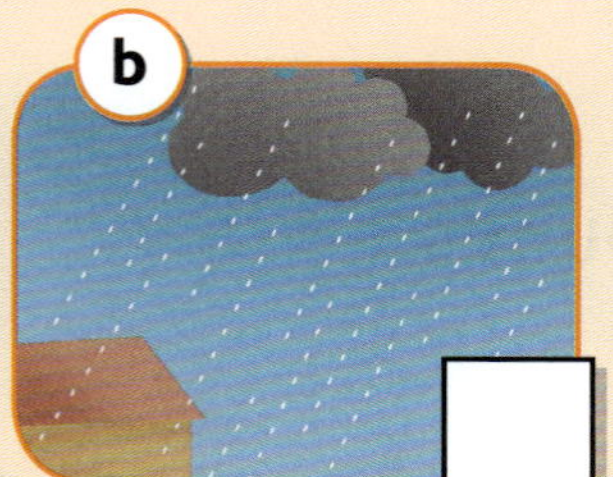

2 a 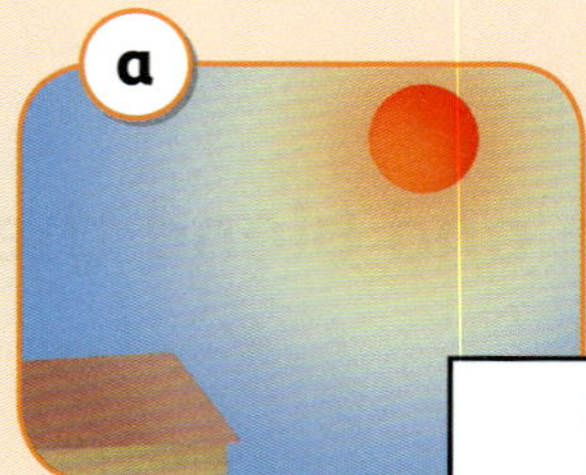 b 

3 a  b 

4 a  b 

25 C:22 Listen. Then play.

26 C:23 Listen and act.

Now go to Poptropica English World

Review Units 7 and 8

1 Read and write the number.

a

b

c

d

1 I'm wearing a sweater and jeans.

2 I'm wearing pants and a hat.

3 I'm wearing a skirt and socks.

4 I'm wearing a T-shirt and pants.

2 Listen and number.

C:24

a

b

c

d

3 Write.

1 S _ _ _ _ _	2 M _ _ _ _ _
3 _ _ _ _ d _ _	4 W _ _ _ _ _ _ _ _ _
5 _ _ _ _ s _ _ _	6 F _ _ _ _ _
7 _ a _ _ _ _ _ _ _	

4 Listen and draw. Then write.

C:25

1

It's ____________________.

Let's ____________________.

2

It's ____________________.

Let's ____________________.

3

It's ____________________.

Let's ____________________.

4

It's ____________________.

Let's ____________________.

Goodbye

1 C:26 **Listen, find, and circle.**

2 C:27 **Listen and number.**

a  ☐

b  ☐

c 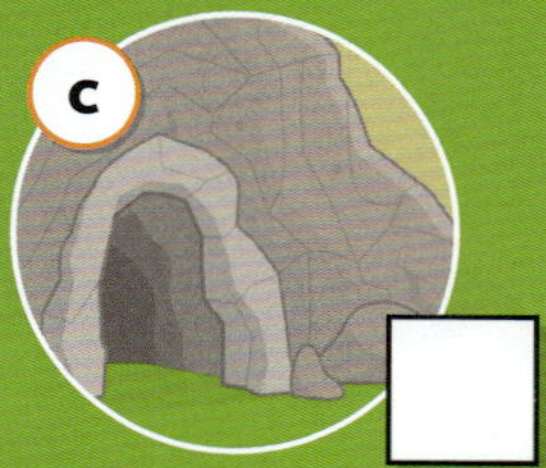 ☐

d 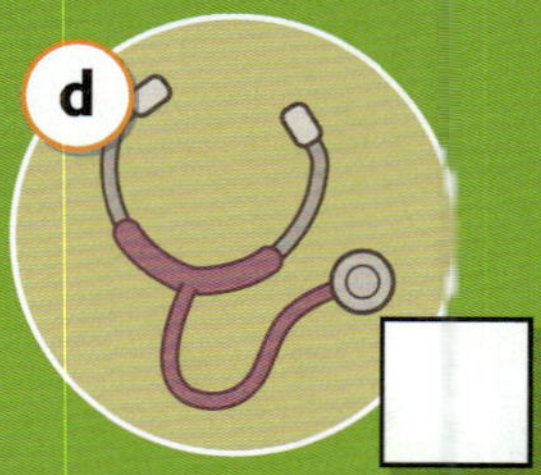 ☐

e  ☐

f  ☐

g  ☐

h  ☐

3 Who is at the party? Write.

1 ____________ 2 ____________ 3 ____________

4 ____________ 5 ____________ 6 ____________

7 ____________ 8 ____________ 9 ____________

4 Listen and number. Then write.

in on under

a

She ________ the cave.

b

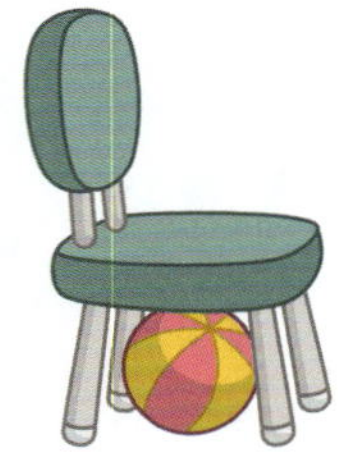

It's ________ the chair.

c

They're ________ the table.

d

He's ________ the castle.

5 Read, look, and circle. Then ask and answer.

1

Where (is / are) the socks?

2

Where (is / are) the doll?

3

Where (is / are) the teddy bear?

4

Where (is / are) the cars?

Where's the teddy bear?

It's in the box.

6 C:29/ C:30 **Listen and sing.**

Stand up, jump up, come on a quest,
Come on a quest today.
Turn around, sit down, come on a quest.
How can we help today?

At the castle, with dinner, at the cave, the doctor, the farmer,
With the shopping, with the clothes, at the mountain
We can help today!

Rose and Charlie are home again,
And Ola's happy today – Hooray!
Rose and Charlie are home again,
And Ola's happy today – Hooray!
Hooray! Hooray! Hooray!
Hooray! Hooray! Hooray!

7 **Draw five of your favorite things. Then show and tell.**

Easter

1 C:31/ C:32 **Make. Then listen and sing.**

Hello, Easter Bunny.
How are you today?
Wake up, wake up,
Come and play.

Jump, jump, jump,
Easter Bunny jump!
Turn around, turn around,
Fall down with a thump.

(x2)

2 **Play the game.**

rabbit

egg

chick

flower

1

1		
2		
3		

2

1		
2		
3		

Can make an Easter Bunny and sing an Easter song

Christmas

1 C:33/C:34 **Listen and sing. Then find and say.**

Hang up your stockings
By the Christmas tree.
Hang up your stockings,
It's Christmas Eve.
It's Christmas Eve.

Who's this with a brown sack
In the living room?
With a long white beard
And a big red nose,
And he laughs with a ho, ho, ho!

Is it true? Can it be?
Yes, It's Santa! Come and see.
With a long white beard
And a big red nose
And presents for you and me.

(Chorus)

2 **Make and play.**

Valentine's Day

1 Listen and sing. Then find and say.

I'm so happy!
Let's sing and play.
I'm so happy!
It's Valentine's Day!

Here's a flower for my mom.
Some chocolates for my dad.
Here's a heart for Grandma,
And a card for Grandpa.

(Chorus)

2 Make and say.

Halloween

1 C:37/ C:38 **Listen and sing. Then find and say.**

Come on! It's Halloween!
It's time to trick-or-treat!
The moon is smiling up there,
And the stars are out there.
Do you have some yummy candy
Ready for me?
Are you a ghost or a scary witch?
Jack-o'-lanterns smile at me!

(x2)

2 **Prepare. Then have a party.**

Wider World 1

Cousins

1 Read and match.

1. This is my uncle and aunt with my cousin Harry. Harry is a baby. They live in Australia!

2. These are my cousins Ella and Jack. Ella is a girl, and Jack is a boy. They are with their parents in this picture. They live in a house.

3. These are my cousins Daisy and Louise. They're twins! They live in an apartment, but in this picture they are in the yard.

4. And this is my cousin Matt. He's eight years old. He lives here in America. He has a treehouse!

a

b

c

d

2 Ask and answer.

How many cousins do you have?

Where do they live?

What are their names?

How old are they?

3 Write about a cousin. How old is he/she? Where does he/she live?

Can understand descriptions of families around the world

Wider World 2

World sports

1 Read and write.

a soccer player

b gymnast

c basketball player

d ballet dancer

e athlete

1 She can do the splits, and she can point her toes. d

2 He can kick a ball, and he can run fast. ☐

3 He can swing and touch his toes. ☐

4 She can run fast, and she can jump. ☐

5 He can catch and throw a ball. He can jump. ☐

2 Play a guessing game.

Can you jump?

Yes, I can.

Can you kick a ball?

Are you an athlete?

No, I can't.

3 Write about a sports person from another country.

Wider World 3

Life on a farm

1 Read and match.

1. My name's Grace. I live in South Africa. I live on an ostrich farm!
2. Ostriches are big birds. They have big bodies and long legs. They can run fast, but they can't fly. The father is black. What color is the mother?
3. These are ostrich eggs. They're very big. How many eggs can you see?
4. These are ostrich chicks. They're funny. What color are they?

a 
b 
c 
d 

2 What farm animals are there in your country? Look and circle.

3 Write about a farm animal in your country. Make a class booklet.

Can understand a simple text about farm animals

Wider World 4

Special clothes

1 Read and check (✓).

When do you wear special clothes?

1 At a birthday party?

2 At a festival?

3 For New Year's?

4 For Halloween?

2 Look, read, and write the numbers.

a My name's Chun. This is me with my friends. I'm wearing black trousers and a white T-shirt. We have a dragon puppet! [ ]

b My name's Olivia. It's my birthday! I'm wearing a pretty pink dress. [ ]

c My name's Brandon, and this is my friend Michael. I'm wearing a white shirt and a black hat. We have pumpkins! [ ]

d I'm Takumi. This is me and my sister. Her name's Ami. I'm wearing a long brown skirt and a coat. Ami is wearing a blue dress with white shoes. 2

3 Ask and answer.

When do you wear special clothes?

What do you wear?

4 Design some special clothes. Make a class booklet.

Picture dictionary

Numbers

16 sixteen

17 seventeen

18 eighteen

19 nineteen

20 twenty

30 thirty

40 forty

50 fifty

Days of the week

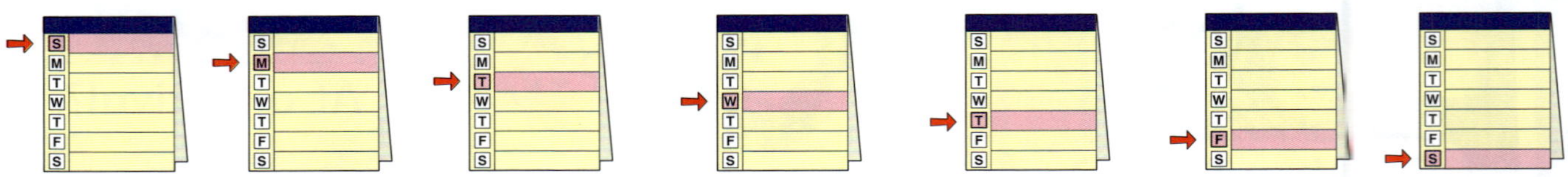

Sunday Monday Tuesday Wednesday Thursday Friday Saturday

Time

one o'clock

two o'clock

three o'clock

four o'clock

five o'clock

six o'clock

seven o'clock

eight o'clock

nine o'clock

ten o'clock

eleven o'clock

twelve o'clock

a

apartment
p. 24

apples
p. 66

aunt
p. 22

b

bakery
p. 24

ball
p. 12

bananas
p. 66

bat
p. 58

beans
p. 68

bike
p. 12

blond
p. 46

boat
p. 12

boots
p. 80

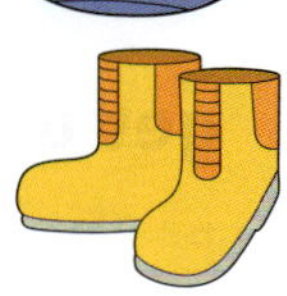

burgers
p. 66

c

cap
p. 80

car
p. 12

cereal
p. 68

chicken
p. 56

chicken
p. 66

climb
p. 36

cloudy
p. 88

coat
p. 80

coconut
p. 68

cool
p. 88

corn
p. 68

cousin 
p. 22

cow 
p. 56

crow 
p. 58

curly 
p. 46

d

dance 
p. 36

dark 
p. 46

daughter 
p. 22

do cartwheels 
p. 36

do the splits 
p. 36

doll 
p. 12

dress 
p. 78

duck 
p. 56

e

ears 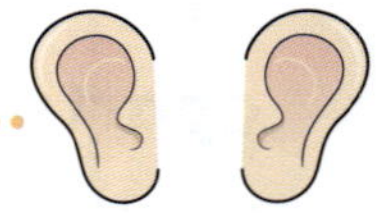
p. 44

eat breakfast 
p. 10

eat dinner 
p. 10

eat lunch 
p. 10

eggs 
p. 66

eyes 
p. 44

f

face 
p. 44

fish 
p. 68

fly a kite 
p. 90

fox 
p. 58

g

get up 
p. 10

goat p. 56

go for a walk p. 90

go to bed p. 10

go to school p. 10

go to the beach p. 90

goose p. 56

granddaughter p. 22

grandson p. 22

grapes p. 68

h

hair p. 44

hat p. 80

horse p. 56

hot dogs p. 66

house p. 24

i

j

jeans p. 80

jump p. 36

k

kite p. 12

l

long p. 46

m

make a snowman p. 90

messy p. 46

mouth p. 44

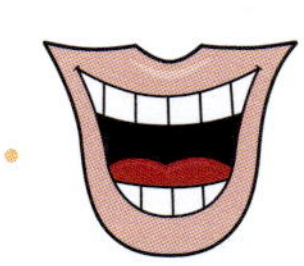

move ....
p. 34

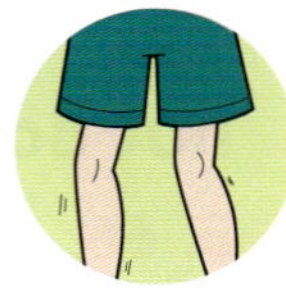

n

neat ....
p. 46

nod ....
p. 34

nose ....
p. 44

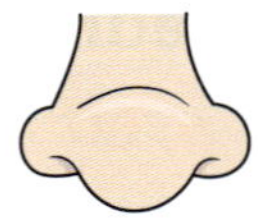

nuts ....
p. 68

o

owl ....
p. 58

p

pajamas ....
p. 80

pants ....
p. 78

pig ....
p. 56

pineapple ....
p. 68

pizza ....
p. 66

point ....
p. 34

post office ....
p. 24

pumpkin ....
p. 68

q

r

rainy ....
p. 88

raisins ....
p. 68

read a book ....
p. 90

restaurant ....
p. 24

rice ....
p. 66

ride a bike ....
p. 90

s

shake ....
p. 34

sheep ....
p. 56

shirt .... p. 80

shoes .... p. 78

short .... p. 46

shorts .... p. 80

sit down .... p. 34

skirt .... p. 78

skunk .... p. 58

sneakers .... p. 80

snowy .... p. 88

socks .... p. 78

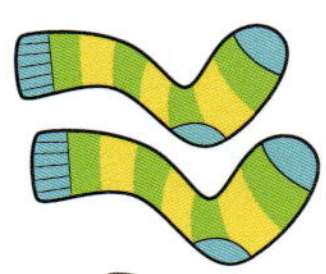

son .... p. 22

stamp .... p. 40

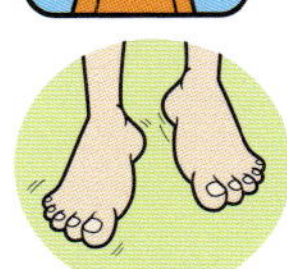

stand on your head .... p. 36

store .... p. 26

straight .... p. 46

sunny .... p. 88

sweater .... p. 80

swim .... p. 36

swing .... p. 36

t

take a picture .... p. 90

teddy bear .... p. 12

toast .... p. 68

touch .... p. 34

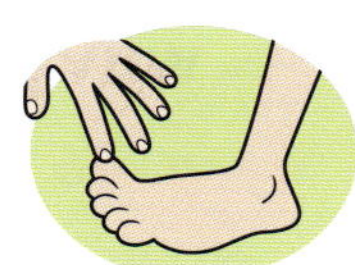

train .... p. 12

truck .... p. 12

T-shirt
p. 78

turkey
p. 56

turn around
p. 34

u

uncle
p. 22

v

w

wake up
p. 10

watch TV
p. 90

wave
p. 34

wavy
p. 46

windy
p. 88

x

y

yard
p. 24

z

Acknowledgments

The Publishers would like to thank the following teachers for their suggestions and comments on this course:

Nurhan Deniz, Alejandra Juarez, Lara Ozer, Cynthia Xu, Basia Zarzycka

Jennifer Dobson, Anabel Higuera Gonzalez, Honorata Klosak, Dr Marianne Nikolov, Regina Ramalho

Asako Abe, JiEun Ahn, Nubia Isabel Albarracín, José Antonio Aranda Fuentes, Juritza Ardila, María del Carmen Ávila Tapia, Ernestina Baena, Marisela Bautista, Carmen Bautista, Norma Verónica Blanco, Suzette Bradford, Rose Brisbane, María Ernestina Bueno Rodríguez, María del Rosario Camargo Gómez, Maira Cantillo, Betsabé Cárdenas, María Cristina Castañeda, Carol Chen, Carrie Chen, Alice Chio, Tina Cho, Vicky Chung, Marcela Correa, Rosalinda Ponce de Leon, Betty Deng, Rhiannon Doherty, Esther Domínguez, Elizabeth Domínguez, Ren Dongmei, Gerardo Fernández, Catherine Gillis, Lois Gu, SoRa Han, Michelle He, María del Carmen Hernández, Suh Heui, Ryan Hillstead, JoJo Hong, Cindy Huang, Mie Inoue, Chiami Inoue, SoYun Jeong, Verónica Jiménez, Qi Jing, Sunshui Jing, Maiko Kainuma, YoungJin Kang, Chisato Kariya, Yoko Kato, Eriko Kawada, Sanae Kawamoto, Sarah Ker, Sheely Ker, Hyomin Kim, Lee Knight, Akiyo Kumazawa, JinJu Lee, Eunchae Lee, Jin-Yi Lee, Sharlene Liao, Yu Ya Link, Marcela Marluchi, Hilda Martínez Rosal, Alejandro Mateos Chávez, Cristina Medina Gómez, Bertha Elsi Méndez, Luz del Carmen Mercado, Ana Morales, Ana Estela Morales, Zita Morales Cruz, Shinano Murata, Junko Nishikawa, Sawako Ogawa, Ikuko Okada, Hiroko Okuno, Tomomi Owaki, Sayil Palacio Trejo, Rosa Lilia Paniagua, MiSook Park, SeonJeong Park, JoonYong Park, María Eugenia Pastrana, Silvia Santana Paulino, Dulce María Pineda, Rosalinda Ponce de León, Liliana Porras, María Elena Portugal, Yazmín Reyes, Diana Rivas Aguilar, Rosa Rivera Espinoza, Nayelli Guadalupe Rivera Martínez, Araceli Rivero Martínez, David Robin, Angélica Rodríguez, Leticia Santacruz Rodríguez, Silvia Santana Paulino, Kate Sato, Cassie Savoie, Mark Savoie, Yuki Scott, Yoshiko Shimoto, Jeehye Shin, MiYoung Song, Lisa Styles, Laura Sutton, Mayumi Tabuchi, Takako Takagi, Miriam Talonia, Yoshiko Tanaka, María Isabel Tenorio, Chioko Terui, José Francisco Trenado, Yasuko Tsujimoto, Elmer Usaguen, Hiroko Usami, Michael Valentine, José Javier Vargas, Nubia Margot Vargas, Guadalupe Vázquez, Norma Velázquez Gutiérrez, Ruth Marina Venegas, María Martha Villegas Rodríguez, Heidi Wang, Tomiko Watanabe, Jamie Wells, Susan Wu, Junko Yamaguchi, Dai Yang, Judy Yao, Yo Yo, Sally Yu, Mary Zhou, Rose Zhuang

Stickers

Unit 1 My toys

page 18

Unit 2 My family

page 24

Unit 3 Move your body

page 39

Unit 4 My face

page 46

Unit 5 Animals

page 58

page 61

Unit 6 Food

page 69

Unit 7 Clothes

page 81

page 83

Good night.	Good morning.	I'm sorry.
Thank you.	Goodbye!	Please.